D. J. SMITH

CW00688575

Discovering
Country Crafts

SHIRE PUBLICATIONS LTD

Contents

ACKNOWLEDGEMENTS

The publishers acknowledge with gratitude the advice of Ivan G. Sparkes and Jacqueline Fearn in the preparation of this book.
Cover design by Ron Shaddock. Line drawings by the author.

Printed in Great Britain by Hunt Barnard Printing Ltd, Aylesbury, Bucks.

1. Basket-making

Basket-making is one of the oldest crafts known to mankind: the
weaving of twigs and grasses for receptacles dates back to at least
5,000 BC. Even the most primitive tribes attempted this form of
work, not only for containers but in the making of boats, rafts,
windbreaks for shelter, and even animal traps.

In Britain the best materials are willow canes, reeds and grasses;
the making of trug baskets and spales from strip wood requires a
slightly different approach. Basket-making was a cottage industry
needing very little space or equipment and so was able to compete
successfully for many years with large-scale factory production.
Although it is possible to weave highly complex patterns, the basic
craft can be taught to young children and has long provided a
means of livelihood for invalids and disabled people who can still
use their hands.

The willows used for most baskets come from osiers, which grow
in marshy country or near riverbanks. Some are imported from
Holland, France, Germany, Poland or the Argentine. Large
quantities, both for home use and export, are cultivated in low-
lying areas of Somerset. Suitable osiers are of low, bushy growth,
pruned to prevent them reaching a great height or turning into
full-sized trees. The growth of the branches or twigs must be
supple, tough and as near uniform length and thickness as
possible. Every twelve months the twigs, known as withies, are
collected and graded into different types suitable for various styles
of work; the coarser and thicker ones are used for larger items.
Both the planting and the harvesting of the osier beds take place
during the early part of the year. Brown rods are usually cut
during the winter and allowed a long period for drying out. Green
rods for cheaper baskets may be cut in the growing season, but
mainly in spring. After harvesting, withies for white baskets are
peeled, while those for buff work are boiled with their bark still on
and peeled when dried.

Normally the basket maker is seated at or near floor level,
surrounded by tools and materials, with an oblong board on his
lap, sometimes known as a *lap board*.

For circular or oval baskets the first part to be made is the
centre-bottom or *slath*. This has an interlaced cross-work of rods,
evenly spaced like wheel spokes. Other withies are woven in and
out of these, until a large enough base is formed. Extra rods are
let in or attached; these are bent upwards to form the uprights.
Weaving is always from left to right. Finer rods are threaded or
woven between the uprights, usually from bottom to top, taking
special care round the *upset* at the base, working to the rim, at
which the uprights are snipped level. Raising the sides is known as
staking up. From time to time the weave of the basket is closed up

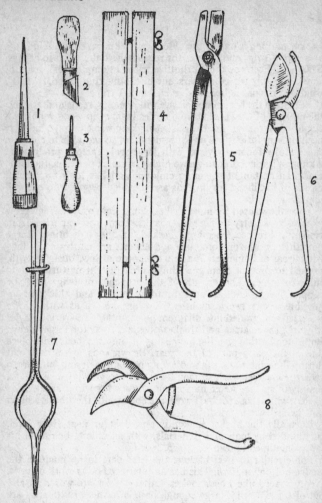

Fig. 1. Basketry tools: 1. large bodkin for making holes to insert rods;
2. pricking knife; 3. bodkin; 4. screw block for clamping in sticks
when making a rectangular lid or base of a basket; 5. kinking shears;
6. shop shears; 7. peeling brake to strip bark from the rods; 8. shears
to cut larger sticks.

with a *driving iron*. Most baskets are woven from bottom to top, although the Yarmouth Swill and the Welsh Gwyntell are made from the rim downwards. Baskets with a square or rectangular bottom have the base made in a wooden form or block, the sides of which are kept screwed together until the last rods are interwoven.

Rush baskets are still made, but in decreasing numbers. Only the bulrush, *Scirpus lacustris,* is used, harvested during late summer and early autumn. They are washed and dried over a period of several weeks. Baskets can be made either by plaiting the reeds into long lengths, which are usually wound around a wooden shape called a *former* and stitched together with string or by interlacing the reeds around the former, holding them in place with drawing pins until the edge is finished with a row of plaiting.

Spales are large but shallow baskets which were used for potato gathering, as coal skips and for many other purposes on the farm. The main centres of production are the Wyre Forest above Bewdley (Hereford and Worcester) and Furness (Cumbria), where a similar basket is known as a *spelk*.

Spales are usually woven from bands or strips of oakwood. The rim is of hazel wood and damp strips are nailed on to form the *ribs* through which *taws* are woven closely to form the container.

Fig. 2. The basket-maker.

Fig. 3. Garden trug (left) and farmer's trug.

Perhaps the most interesting of the many varieties of basket is the trug of Sussex, which is in a category by itself. Thomas Smith of Herstmonceux, who made trug baskets, displayed some of his products on a stand at the Great Exhibition of 1851. These were admired by Queen Victoria, who ordered several. Trugs are normally used for garden work but also make good fruit baskets.

The word *trug* was based on the Old English name for a woven boat or coracle, which is said to have inspired the early designs. The rim and handle of the basket are made from chestnut or ash poles cut lengthways and the frame is of pollard willow. Suitable lengths of strip, called *straps,* are trimmed on a shaving horse with a draw-knife. All straps are steamed for greater flexibility, then moulded to the correct form and attached with copper nails to the

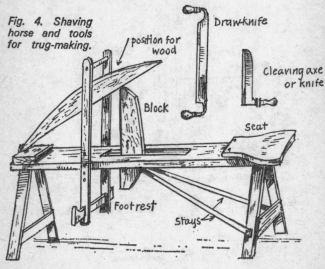

Fig. 4. Shaving horse and tools for trug-making.

position for wood

Draw-knife

Cleaving axe or knife

Block

Seat

Footrest

Stays

rim, which has been shaped around a former. After the bottom slat has been nailed on, the rest slightly overlap each preceding slat until the rim is reached. The large bushel-sized trug, used by farmers, is without a handle and may have diagonal straps on the outside for added support. On standard trugs the handle is attached to the rim before work on the body begins.

Tools for basket-making

These include the peeling brake, shop shears, shop knife (used for trimming baskets), bodkin, long bodkin, pricking knife, clamping block (for making square bottoms), draw-knife and cleaving knife.

The shaving horse for trug-making, mentioned above, is also used in other crafts and has existed for several centuries. It helps to keep the wood in a firm position while leaving the hands free to use the draw-knife or other tools.

Uses for baskets

There are many different types of basket with special uses, although some are now obsolete. The bottle basket, stone-jar basket, umbrella basket for carriages, work basket, lunch basket, angler's basket and floral display basket are only a few of them. Some of the largest baskets were made for loading oil cake in South Africa. Each could hold a ton of cake, the top being nearly six feet in diameter. They were constructed by men sitting inside each basket and working outwards.

2. Thatching

Thatching is a craft practised in many lands. The name derives from the Old English word *thacke*, meaning to roof over or cover. Thatching was used not only for houses, cottages and outbuildings but also to protect ricks of the summer harvest.

The rural thatcher was a very important member of the community, needed at all times of the year, but chiefly in the early autumn when ricks had to be thatched. It has been said that 'thatching is a job many men can do, but few can do well'. It is a craft in which an individual relies far more on practical experience than on knowing a few technical tricks. Even the apparently simple task of straightening straw between the fingers, or *yealming*, may prove difficult to a novice.

Although now less in demand on the farm since the advent of the combine harvester and the decline of rick-making, the craft of house thatching is undergoing a limited revival largely because many thatched cottages have been bought in recent years by people who can afford to rethatch them.

7

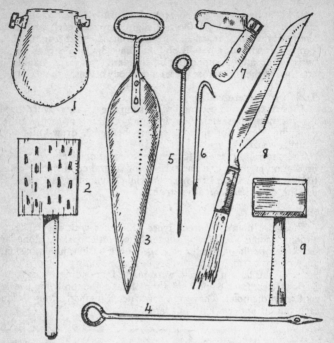

Fig. 5. The tools of the thatcher: 1. knee pad or cap; 2. leggat; 3. opening tool; 4. needle; 5. pin; 6. reed hook; 7. thatcher's clasp-knife; 8. eaves knife; 9. mallet.

Several different materials are used for thatching, including straw, bracken, heather and reeds. Modern thatchers favour straw or reeds, the former being much cheaper but lasting about twenty years less than well selected reeds. The average life of reed thatch is about sixty years. Straw is still the most universal and popular material, especially from wheat, but also from rye. Barley straw is usually too soft in texture and absorbs rather than sheds moisture. The most widespread method is long-straw thatching with ordinary threshed straw. Shallow piles of loose straw are moistened with water and straightened by hand, each handful being taken from the bottom of the heap and assembled into yealms about eighteen inches wide and five inches deep (*yealm* is the Old English for an armful or handful). A straw bond, made of several straws twisted together, is the traditional binding, sometimes now replaced by twine. To make a straw bond an iron crank like the starting handle of a car, known as a *bond twister*,

Fig. 6.
Pattern of
spars
round
eaves.

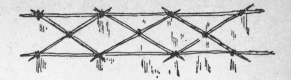

can be used, ideally fed by straws pulled from the face of the rick.
Lengths of straw are threaded through the crook of the twister and
through a further grip halfway along the shaft. The bond is woven
by twisting and rotating about seven straws round the crank while
moving backwards, away from the rick. Most thatchers can make
a bond, at least a yard or so in length, within a few minutes.

The thatcher needs plenty of pegs, or *spars*. These, driven firmly
into the straw, pack the thatch close on the roof or rick and are
made of hazel or withy twigs. Rods about four feet in length and
an inch or two in diameter are split with a *spar hook,* which has a
short blade kept at razor sharpness. The split sections are twisted
in the centre and then bent to form a staple shape. Shorter spars
are used for buildings and longer spars for ricks. Before use the
spars are soaked in water for a day or two, which enables them to
be worked without cracking. In most cases the spar or peg is
pointed at both ends but in some areas pointed only at one end.
They have been compared to giant hairpins or grips, known,
according to local usage, as spars, spies, pegs, pins, tangs or
withynecks. Long rods of hazel called *sways* are needed to hold the
thatch in place and thinner rods for the external liggers at eaves
and ridge.

When thatching a rick, spars are pushed into the rick
horizontally or slightly upward and toughened twine, soaked in
tar, is looped and stitched over the yealms, between the spars,
beginning near the eaves and working along the roof of the rick in
parallel lines from top to bottom. Bonded straw may also be used
for this purpose. Twine is sewn with a large iron needle.

*Fig. 7. Thatched corn stacks: (left) northern English; (centre)
southern English; (right) cut stack covered by sheets.*

9

In Wales ricks are frequently thatched without spars, the straw being covered and held in place with a net of twine, weighted at the bottom with large stones. This is found to be more secure than ordinary thatching in exposed areas subject to storms. Some houses and cottages near the coast are also roofed in this way.

The thatching of a roof begins at the bottom and usually moves from right to left, ending at the ridge. Great care is taken to avoid leaving gaps uncovered overnight, and a good thatcher always completes his final *strake* or section before stopping work.

The first yealms (which are called bottles at the eaves, are wider and splayed at the large end) may be either tied in with a cord stapled into the corner of the eaves or secured by a sway held down by hooks driven into the rafters. Each bottle is driven hard against the previous one, intermingling, with spars driven horizontally from left to right into the straw before the sway is finally secured. After a double course at the eaves succeeding courses are laid overlapping the lower by two thirds. The straw is constantly pushed tight between thatching needles driven temporarily into the rafters. A form of wooden rake is used to comb out loose straw. Some men also use wooden mallets for driving in the spars (these are never used on ricks). The surface of the finished work and the edges of the eaves are trimmed with shears and a special long-handled knife. Along the top of the roof a ridge or capping is laid based on long rolls of straw placed along the ridge board. The ridge courses are secured by long hazel rods called *liggers* which also provide a basis for whatever decorative pattern the thatcher wishes to make on the finished ridge. He will add liggers along the eaves after trimming the thatch.

It is in the ridging and other finishing touches that the thatcher is seen as an individual and an artist. Some thatchers are able to work intricate patterns in the straw, known as dog's tooth or hound's tooth, while edgings may be *tongued*, giving them alternating depths and levels. The general aim is to contrast these intricate patterns with a bold sweep of curves, round porches and gables, with the eaves neatly trimmed to emphasise the character of each line and contour. There was formerly a tradition in some parts of the country for adding straw ornaments to the roof ridge, similar to corn dollies: where the practice persists it tends to be a trademark for the thatcher.

An important part of the thatcher's work, especially as a trainee or apprentice, is to gauge the amount of straw required for a particular roof or rick. Houses and cottages vary in size but the average rick required one hundred yealms and a *bundle* of two hundred and fifty spars. Spars are counted by the bundle. The experienced craftsman depends very much on hand and eye, needing few measurements. He can usually tell at a glance, when inspecting the site, how many yealms and bundles are needed.

Reed thatching, popular in the eastern counties, is a branch of the craft that not all straw thatchers are able to tackle or manage well. It is more durable than straw and has a neat and pleasing finish but is more costly than other roofing materials. The best reeds for this purpose are grown and harvested in the eastern counties, especially the Norfolk reed.

Unlike straw thatchers, who work on one side at a time in careful strakes, reed thatchers work all round the roof to a depth of two feet (but always from right to left), adding further layers as the work progresses. Once the reeds are firmly secured by sway hooks the butt ends are beaten upwards with a tool known as a *leggat*, which appears similar to a bat with raised studs on the under surface. The Devonshire leggat, also used in other parts of the West Country, has grooves in place of studs. Some thatchers also use a much smaller leggat with a looped or shoebrush handle for awkward places and corners. Using a leggat ensures an even, continuous and slightly bristled surface. Many thatchers, especially for reed work, wear an iron sheath on one arm, known as an *opening tool*. This resembles a pointed scoop and is useful for probing into and behind the thatch.

Combed wheat-reed thatching, which is similar in technique to Norfolk-reed thatching, uses a long unthreshed wheat stalk, formerly known as Devon reed. This is better than ordinary wheat straw but not as weatherproof as the finest reeds, although similar in texture. At one time the straw underwent a costly process of sorting and combing, mainly done by the women of the village. In more recent years the same process was mechanised by passing the straws through the comber of a threshing box.

There are now about seven hundred and fifty full-time thatchers in different parts of England and Wales. They work in straw and reeds, often travelling long distances to practise their highly decorative craft. In farming there is very little work to be done as both threshing and the making of ricks has greatly diminished. The combine harvester, which has replaced the reaper-binder, now threshes as it cuts, and the abandoned straw is collected by a baling machine that turns out neatly shaped bales of straw bound with wires; these are stacked under plastic covers or tarpaulins and rarely suitable for thatching. This means that the long-straw thatcher has lost both his work on the farm and the straw he needs for thatching generally; his supplies have to be specially harvested without the use of the baler. Similarly the straw for combed wheat reed is supplied to order and specially processed through the reed comber attached to the threshing drum.

3. Saddlery and harness-making

Saddlery and harness-making were once separate crafts, especially in towns, but now they are usually carried on in the same workshop. The village saddler and harness-maker was a much valued figure in the days of horse transport, most of his work relating to farm horses and the making or repairing of their harness. During the greater part of the nineteenth century, however, the wealthier people tended to deal with craftsmen or firms, often of international repute, in the large towns.

Mechanisation began to reduce the need for saddlers and harness-makers towards the end of the nineteenth century. The steam railways were at first complementary to the horse, for

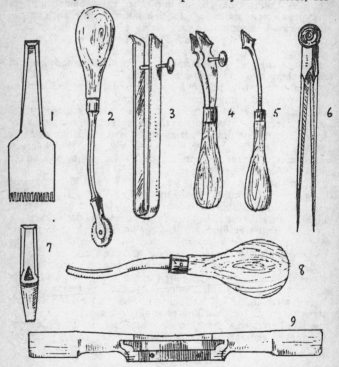

Fig. 8. Tools of the saddler and harness-maker; 1. pricking iron; 2. wheel pricker or pricking wheel; 3. screw race; 4. double or screw crease; 5. single crease; 6. compasses; 7. punch; 8. edge trimmer; 9. spokeshave.

although stagecoaches began to decline from the 1850s, there was still a demand for horse-drawn station buses, cabs and delivery vehicles as the railway could never offer a door-to-door service. Between 1860 and 1900, even with express trains travelling at a speed of a mile a minute, the horse continued to hold its own, supporting a large number of craftsmen serving its needs.

R. E. Whiting, Past Master of the Worshipful Company of Saddlers, in his introduction to a reprint of the classic *Saddlery and Harness Making* by P. N. Hasluck states that the peak of the harness trade was in 1904. Main roads between larger centres were fairly quiet and traffic-free but the streets of towns and villages echoed to the sound of many hooves, for horses were generally used for short hauls, the motorcar then being little more than a

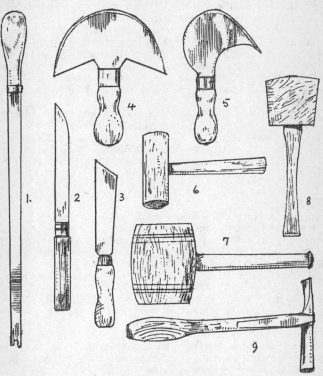

Fig. 9. Tools of the saddler and harness-maker: 1. stuffing stick; 2. paring knife; 3. hand knife; 4. round knife; 5. head knife; 6, 7 and 8. wooden mallets; 9. saddler's hammer.

fad for a few wealthy people. It is significant, however, that, while at the beginning of 1905 the London General Omnibus Company had only twenty motor vehicles, they increased this to two hundred by the end of the year.

During the early 1920s there was a serious slump amongst saddlers, harness-makers and farriers in both town and country, although riding for pleasure, hunting and racing kept a certain number of craftsmen in regular work. By 1939 there were eighteen hundred saddlers left in England and Wales, and by the early 1960s this number had fallen to well below one thousand. In recent years there has been a revival of riding for pleasure, but this gain has been offset by a great increase in farm tractors during the 1960s. There is still work for the local craftsman during the 1980s but this is mainly connected with equestrian sports, pony clubs, private riding and driving and only a very small amount of farm work. Some saddlers and harness-makers also spend a considerable part of their time making or selling hand luggage and general sports goods. Saddlery and harness-making are still traditional crafts depending on skill of hand and judgement of eye. It would not be practical to mechanise this type of work and the tools of the trade may well have been used for a great many years.

The combined crafts may be divided into three parts: saddlery, harness-making, and the making of neck collars for draught work — both heavy and light. All three require special skills, a long apprenticeship and, at one time, long hours for very little money. Much of the work is not only difficult and painstaking, but highly intricate.

Saddlery

Numerous types of saddles for different purposes have evolved throughout history — for hunting, military purposes, ladies riding side-saddle, children on small ponies, and even pack saddles for merchandise. Some, especially those for ladies or showing purposes, were highly decorative; others were strictly functional. All types are based on a sound *tree* of beechwood and metal, covered with leather and padded internally.

The most popular type, which was also the traditional saddle of Europe, called the gentleman's riding saddle, was made for the normal astride seat and is now modified as the general-purpose saddle. This has a fairly high and rounded part at the rear, known as the *cantle*. The fore part, also known as the *gullet*, could be either straight or slanting backwards according to taste. There were a number of variations on the main theme, in style, materials and workmanship. Stirrup leathers were attached to the saddle bars or metal parts of the tree. These again were subject to several patent or traditional designs. The lower parts of the flaps

14

hung either forwards or in a straight line from the front of the tree.

The modern saddle is based on a traditional skeleton or tree of laminated beechwood, having a low cantle with two steel spring-plates and stirrup brackets of forged steel. Padded sections or pads are fitted directly under each saddle, resting on the back of

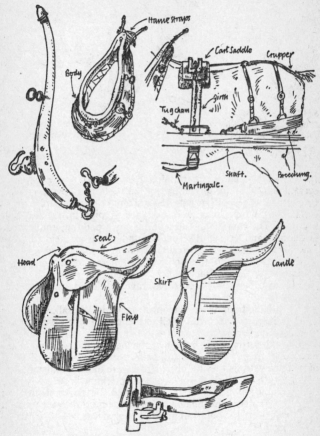

Fig. 10. Details of harness and saddles: (top left) hame; (top centre) draught collar; (top right) draught harness; (lower left) modern saddle; (lower right) gentleman's riding saddle, 1890s; (bottom) saddle tree.

Fig. 11. Fitting the skirts of a saddle.

the horse. The padding material may be flock or wool covered by serge, linen or, preferably, calfskin. The material of the skirts (just below the seat, on either side of the front or head) is pigskin or calfskin, while the seat and flaps are of pigskin, grained side upwards. The cushion of the seat has flock padding under strips of webbing and a cover of serge. The under pads are held firmly in place by four steel rivets, two at the front and two at the back. The saddle is secured to the body of the horse by means of an adjustable girth. Special saddles are made for racing, hunting, showing and other purposes. An average saddle weighs about eight kilograms.

Most saddle trees are now manufactured in Walsall, which has been an important centre for all branches of the trade for many years.

After the cutting and shaping of the leather, the webbing of the seat and stuffing of the seat and pads, perhaps the most difficult part of the work is the stitching. Holes have to be equidistant and close together, marked out with a pricking iron or wheel. Considerable judgement is also needed in the selection of materials for use, knowing how to relate the most durable parts of a hide or skin to the points of greatest wear and tear.

Harness

Harness for light work and smaller vehicles differs from that for heavy work with drays and wagons. Bridles or head pieces for heavy draught work are much sturdier than those used for riding purposes, and have, in addition, large *blinkers,* also known as *winkers* or eye pieces, which prevent a draught horse from being disturbed by the sight of its following vehicle.

Most harness is in three parts: the collar (which is often the work of a specialist); the cart saddle or pad, which takes the weight of the draught gear or shafts; and the leather straps, including the broad band of the breeching, with hip straps, which join other parts together and prevent a load straining the hind quarters when going downhill. Breeching became unfashionable for light harness horses during the second half of the nineteenth century.

The cart saddle, like a riding saddle, is built on a wooden tree and stuffed or lined, usually with straw. There is a grooved ridge in the centre of the saddle, over and through which a ridge chain is hung, connecting with metal loops on the shafts. The saddle is

Fig. 12. Driving harness for a single light horse (used with trap, float, spring cart, gig, etc): A. crown piece; B. browband; C. V-straps; D. rosette; E. blinkers; F. cheek strap or cheek piece; G. noseband; H. throatlash; I. bit (Liverpool); J. reins; K. collar; L. girth; M. trace; N. hooking-in chain; O. driving rings; P. trace bar and ring; Q. breeching; R. breeching strap; S. shaft tug; T. terrets; U. split cross strap; V. crupper; W. quarter strap; X. back strap; Y. hip or loin strap; Z. bellyband.

held in place by a broad girth-strap that fits round the belly of the horse. The *crupper* is a short back strap, through which the tail is looped, attached to the meeter strap, in turn attached to the saddle or pad. Trace harness, used for an extra horse or trace horse (sometimes known as a chain horse) attached in tandem to the shaft horse, has a smaller pad in place of the cumbersome cart saddle, with single rather than double hip straps, worn without breeching. *Trace chains* lead from the tug hooks on the hames of the neck collar to trace hooks on the shafts or other parts of the vehicle to be drawn.

Collars

In Britain the most popular form of collar was the neck or standard draught collar. This was sometimes replaced, especially for light, swift military work, such as in the gun teams of the Royal Horse Artillery, by a breast collar, a type more widely used in continental countries. The neck collar was said to be more suitable for the neck and shoulder conformation of English draught horses and is certainly better for heavy harness work. Most of the pull or push of the draught horse is through the collar, which has attachments for trace hooks and rein rings.

Each collar is made to suit the type of horse for which it was intended and great care has to be taken in fitting and adjustment

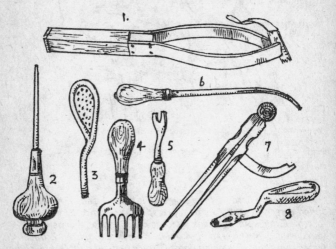

Fig. 13. Tools of the saddler and harness-maker: 1. wooden clamp or vice; 2. sewing awl; 3. palm iron; 4. straining fork; 5. nail claw; 6. steel seat iron; 7. race compasses; 8. palm iron.

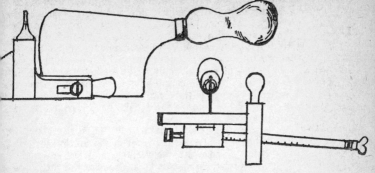

Fig. 14. Plough-gauge: (left) side elevation; (right) end elevation.

so that it lies snug on the neck and shoulders but leaves clear the top of the neck and the throat. A badly fitting collar may soon cause neck galls. Collar-making starts with the *wale*, which is a tube of leather stuffed with rye straw. The tightly packed roll is put round a collar block shaped like the horse's neck and the body of the collar is stitched to it. This can be all leather or have serge on the inside and is tightly stuffed with straw and flock; then the edges are stitched together. Metal bars or *hames* are fixed between the wale and the body in grooves on either side of the collar, each bar joined at the lower front by a chain. Upper parts of the hames curve slightly outwards, rising well above the top of the collar, joined by leather hamestraps. The points of the hames were often, but not always, decorated. They have a pair of rings to take the reins and a pair of tug hooks to take the trace chains. A leather strap or *martingale* attaches the lower part of the neck collar, between the legs, to the girth. This is fairly broad and used to be hung with traditional brasses, some dating in design from pagan times and believed to ward off the evil eye.

In making the neck collar, reeds or straws for stuffing were packed into the tube, between wale and body, by means of an iron rod or bar. Before the final stitching the collar was beaten or moulded into shape on a block.

Equipment for the saddler and harness-maker

There are many items used by the saddler and harness-maker and sometimes these have regional variations. They include various types of needle, collar stuffing mallets, stuffing sticks or rods, palm irons, stitch wheels, pricking irons, punches, a *compass race* and a *half-moon knife* — essential to all leather-workers. Some craftsmen use an instrument known as a *plough-gauge*,

19

which is pushed with the right hand while the leather is held in the left hand. This is useful for making straight leather straps or rolls up to six inches in gauge.

Stitching is done with a number of different-sized needles, ranging from the small sailmaker's needle, about two and a half inches long, to the waling needle, eight inches long. These are usually curved and of round, diamond or crescent section. The protective thimble of the saddler and harness-maker is the hand or *palm iron*, firmly gripped in the centre of the hand; it has a skew hole through which the point of the needle may be pulled and a recess through which it may be pressed or pushed.

The line of stitching is marked out on the leather with a rotating stitch wheel, which has a range of wheel heads for spacing out different-sized holes and widths between them. Some craftsmen use a pricking iron for this purpose. Straps or pieces of leather to be sewn together are held in a special wooden vice or clamp.

The *compass race* or race compasses are used for marking out grooves in leather, along edges, taking out a narrow strip on the grain side. Ordinary compasses, similar to dividers, are used for marking out widths.

Various iron rods with long shafts and pronged ends are used to push stuffing into collars and saddles. The pummelling of the outer collar requires a small mallet of lignum vitae.

Indentations for straps and other leathers, mainly along borders and outer edges, are made with a metal *creasing iron*, which has screw-adjusted jaws or blades and is heated before use. There are double and single creasing irons and a U-shaped screw race used for making indentations for deep stitching.

Various hammers, mallets, awls and punches, mainly for making holes, are self-explanatory.

---

4. The wheelwright and wagon-builder

In the heyday of horse transport the wheelwright, the farrier and the harness-maker worked as a team. Although his main work was connected with the making and repairing of wheels, a trained wheelwright would also be able to construct wagons and other farm vehicles, as required. Such wagons were made to last and if kept in good repair would outlast several generations.

The coach seems to have been introduced into the British Isles as late as the sixteenth century but from the seventeenth until the nineteenth century poorer people and their goods were carried between the towns by stage-wagons and carrier's wagons. These lumbering vehicles, protected from the weather by canvas-covered hoops, were drawn by teams of eight or more horses, but the

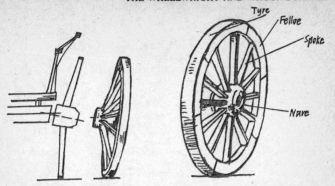

Fig. 15. (Left) Dished wheels, cross-section and backview. (Right) Parts of a wheel.

service came to a halt during the winter months because of deep mire, flooding and snowdrifts on the badly made roads. They were without effective braking, springing or underlock, but of sound and sturdy build, usually the pride of local craftsmen. They carried both passengers and goods and, even after the introduction of stage and mail coaches, were considered both cheaper and safer than the so-called 'flyers', certainly less likely to crash or overturn. For many years the stage-wagon was known as 'the poor man's stagecoach'.

The most important part of either vehicle was the wheel, on which both safety and efficiency depended. Most wheels for horse-drawn vehicles were dished — the spokes sloped slightly outwards from the hub — which enabled the wheel to absorb sideways thrust, uphold the weight and stand clear of the side. Wheels varied in rim width and were tyred either with *strakes,* long sections of metal nailed to the rim, overlapping the joints, or with hoops, which completely encircled the wheel and were fitted red-hot.

Carts have been used in Britain since the fourth century BC at least, in one variation or another, on the simple principle of two wheels on a single axle carrying the weight of the body. They were suitable for most sorts of terrain, needed one animal to haul and tipped naturally to discharge the load. Like wagons they differed in style regionally, had strongly panelled sides or bodies, broad-tyred wheels, and rudimentary braking. When at rest, however, all vehicles could be made immovable by propsticks, dog sticks and scotch rollers (under the wheels).

Farm wagons gradually acquired local characteristics in different parts of the country and by the mid eighteenth century it

Prop Stick.

Strakes

Fig. 16. A tumbril.

Fig. 17. A Cotswold wagon.

was possible to distinguish between a Cotswold wagon, a Herefordshire wagon, an East Yorkshire wagon and many other types. These were all within the competence of the village wheelwright and his men, with a little help from the blacksmith. Light passenger vehicles, carriages for the gentry and stagecoaches, however, were usually made in towns and cities, especially London, although Liverpool and Wolverhampton also acquired a reputation in this sphere by the mid nineteenth century.

During the second half of the nineteenth century local wagons and carts were still being made in large numbers, but there was also a challenge from town firms producing cheaper, factory-made products, which were certainly neither as attractive nor as enduring as those of the local craftsmen. Local men were eventually reduced to cheaper competitive workmanship, or the making and repairing of wheels, which may have been their original function. Even if motor vehicles and tractors had not ousted the horse-drawn wagon, factory competition would have greatly reduced the number of small craftsmen needed by this trade.

The most important feature of wagon-building and the craft of the wheelwright was to procure the right quality wood, well seasoned and sawn into manageable lengths. At one time many local craftsmen had their own sawpits, although very few of these survived into the period after the First World War.

Elm was used for wheel naves, secured on the outside with iron bands or hoops. It was only elm that would stand up to the mortising of between ten and fourteen wheel spokes in the same small compass. Oak and ash were used for the framework of the bodies and elm for the cross panelling and floorboards. Rails and extension ladders, to contain or support overhanging parts of the load, and likely to take hard knocks, were made from ash, noted for its springy qualities and extra resilience. Wheel spokes were of oak and *felloes* (pronounced 'fellies' in some parts), or segments of the outer wheel, were of ash, elm or beech.

However complex the craft of wagon-building, wheels were the mainstay of business, as a good vehicle outlasted several sets of wheels: local reputations were founded on their soundness and durability. *Naves,* in the centres of the wheels, were lathed, bound with iron hoops, then hollowed out or mortised for the spokes by using *buzz, auger* and chisel. The ends of the spokes to fit the mortice holes were cut and the spokes driven into the nave. The shoulders for the tongues on the outer ends of the spokes were shaped, round or square, to fit into the felloes, two spokes fitting into each felloe. A dowel was fitted between the felloes to keep the circle. Wheel spokes were fashioned with a draw-knife and spokeshave and finished with sandpaper, the felloes latterly cut on

Fig. 18. Making spoke holes.

a bandsaw but earlier shaped with an adze. With straked wheels the lengths of iron were in double bands, side by side. Joints between the bands were staggered on a dished wheel, so as to meet midway between joints of the felloes.

Hoop or band tyres had to be of exact measurements, otherwise they would crack the wheel or work loose, with disastrous results. The length of iron was first marked to the correct dimensions with a measuring instrument known as a *traveller*. The cut strip, allowing for overlap in expansion through heating, was put through rollers and then welded to form a band. The tyre was heated until red-hot, then rapidly dropped into position around the rim of the wheel, now clamped on an iron tyring platform — there was an aperture in the centre of the platform into which the hub or nave of the wheel was fixed by means of an iron screw rod and turnkey. Once the tyre was in position it was forced home by

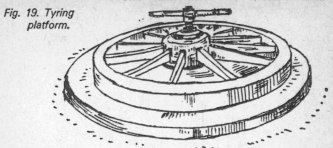

Fig. 19. Tyring platform.

men working with sledgehammers. As the tyre cooled, buckets of water were poured over it to speed up the cooling process and to prevent the wooden parts from catching fire. The action of cooling bonded the wheel structure far more firmly than could have been achieved by blows of the hammer alone; this was a further advantage of the band tyre over strakes and the even earlier iron studs.

Old-style carts and wagons had axletrees made of hardened beechwood, from which arms projected, slightly downwards and outwards, fitted with iron cleats and tapering towards the ends. In more recent years metal arms, case-hardened, were bolted to the wooden framework in the centre. These were much lighter, cheaper and perhaps more effective than wooden arms, although this is a matter over which wagoners and wheelwrights do not always agree.

In the construction of both wheels and wagons an important part of the craft was known as *chamfering*. This was done by cutting and bevelling along outer edges both to save weight and to improve the overall appearance. It is said that by skilful bevelling an eighth of the original weight of the wagon could be shaved away, without affecting its strength and durability. Patterns of chamfering varied in different parts of the country, as did the colour schemes, lettering styles and decoration of the headboards.

Although wagons were used in most parts of Britain they were less frequently seen in highland districts such as Scotland, Central Wales, the Pennines and Cornwall; these hilly areas were best served by carts, which were lighter and more manoeuvrable. Britain could thus be divided into wagon country and cart country, and there were very few wagons north of the Scottish border, unless imported by English families. In Wales four-wheeled farm vehicles were restricted to the south-east, the coastal plains and some of the broader, more fertile valleys.

Tools the wheelwright needed include the spokeshave, bow saw, *boxing engine* or *screw rod* and *turnkey, traveller, spoke tenon*

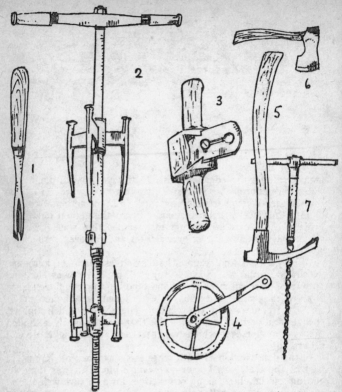

Fig. 20. Tools of the wheelwright: 1. buzz; 2. screw rods or boxing engine; 3. jarvis; 4. traveller; 5. adze; 6. axe; 7. auger.

cutter, jarvis, shell auger (for boring), *buzz, tenon cutter* and *spoke rounder*. In some more up-to-date yards, from the 1900s, a machine known as a *tyring press* was used. This was a hydraulic press and could be used for tyres up to forty inches in diameter, but not for the larger wheels of farm wagons and carts. It was also limited to a tyre width of one and a half inches.

5. The blacksmith and farrier

As with the saddler and harness-maker, wheelwright and wagon-builder, the blacksmith and the farrier followed originally separate crafts which became closely allied and were often undertaken by the same person, especially in a small community. The blacksmith was a general worker in iron and heavy metals, at his own forge, while the farrier shod horses and was also known as a shoeing smith. Both crafts are of great antiquity and often use similar tools and techniques. The word *smith* probably came from the Old English word *smite,* used in association with the striking of iron. *Farrier* derived from the Norman-French word *ferier,* or ironworker. It eventually became associated with those given the care of the feet of horses and the fitting of iron shoes. At an even later period the farrier was also a horse doctor or person looking after the well-being of horses and mules, especially in the army. There were farriers in every cavalry regiment, those in the Household Cavalry being known as Farrier Major, Farrier Corporal and Farrier Corporal of Horse. The last often appears on parade with a ceremonial poleaxe, mistaken by many laymen for a battleaxe. This was used after a battle for the humane killing of horses too badly wounded to recover.

The village smith not only shod horses but also provided most of the metal tools and implements needed in a village or country

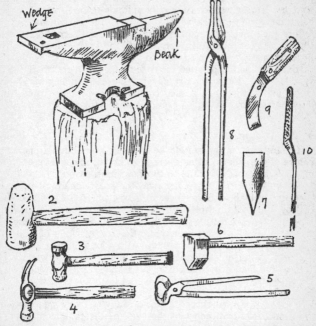

Fig. 21. Tools of the blacksmith and farrier: 1. anvil; 2. sledgehammer; 3. catshead hammer; 4. shoeing hammer; 5. pincers; 6. cold set; 7. head of a pritchell; 8. tongs; 9. paring knife; 10. file or rasp.

district, working in iron, bronze and various other metals. His forge was often an important meeting place and centre of village life. The smith was an important and indispensable member of the community, turning his hand to making items as diverse as swords and pruning hooks, pot hangers, fire bars and door hinges.

From the fifteenth to the early nineteenth centuries the local smith often made metal scrollwork and ornaments, from elaborate gates for the lord of the manor to simple wall hooks and brackets used in the smallest cottage in the village. Some of these works were of great beauty, especially when seen in churches as part of an ornamental grille or hinges on double doors.

There were very few smiths unable to shoe a horse, although a full-time farrier would be the specialist. The greatest demand for farriers and shoeing smiths was during the period from the seventeenth century until the late nineteenth century, but there was a gradual decline from the 1900s with the increased use of motor transport. In the early days of motoring, however, the smith might also be expected to handle simple repairs on cars and early tractors. Horses were not the only animals to be shod, as mules, asses and oxen were also widely used on the land until the second half of the nineteenth century. The magnificent farm horses were the mainstay of the country farrier until the 1930s. Modern smiths have in many cases returned to ornamental work, while the farrier's business is devoted to those riding for pleasure. There is still, however, some military shoeing in ceremonial units of the army, and farriers are needed by the large brewery firms using dray horses, and in hunting and racing stables.

The blacksmith's shop

The forge or smithy would be a large shed-like building near the centre of the village, often facing the green, and partly open on one side, at least during the hours of daylight.

The most distinctive feature was the hearth made of brick or masonry, well above floor level and measuring in the region of five feet by four feet by three feet six inches. Above the hearth was a large metal hood leading to the flue. Behind the hearth or beside it was a set of bellows, for keeping up the fire by means of draught. This was operated by a hand-pump with a long handle, its grip in the form of an upward-turned cow's horn. The fire was stoked with a long-handled shovel known as a *slice*. At one side of the hearth would be a deep metal tank, set in the brickwork or quite near, kept at least two thirds filled with clean water. This was used for cooling and quenching the work. Many of the forge tools were hung on a rod or bracket at the back of the tank, while others would hang from a low roof beam.

At one period blacksmiths and farriers made a number of their own tools and smaller items, especially tongs. The larger implements such as anvils and sledges were supplied by specialist firms.

The anvil normally occupied a central position on the shop floor, raised on a wooden block of oak or elm. This support was necessary to give life to the anvil, which would otherwise seem flat and dead, less responsive to the craftsman's touch. The modern anvil was perfected in England during the middle ages. Like the earlier Roman anvil it had a flat, square or rectangular surface ending in a wedge at one end: the opposite end was pointed and conical, an innovation of the thirteenth century. Such an anvil weighs two hundredweights or more and, when struck with a metal tool, produces a fine ringing sound, almost like a bell.

When the horse is brought into the forge it is allowed to stand for a few minutes, to accustom itself to unfamiliar noises, sights and odours. A young horse is often taken to the forge with an older, more experienced animal, which is shod first.

The farrier starts by examining all the hooves in turn, starting with the forefeet. A vicious or highly nervous horse might have to be cast or felled for shoeing, as oxen often were when they were shod for road work. In some parts of the Continent and in the army the farrier used a framework or stocks to hold the horse fairly still, unable to lash out. Preliminary work on the hoof is sometimes done by an assistant or second man, known in some parts of the country as the doorman. Old nails are first removed with strong pincers and the clinches knocked off with a *buffer*, a double-ended chisel used with a hammer. Each hoof is then cleaned, pared and rasped; the cleaning is done with the pointed

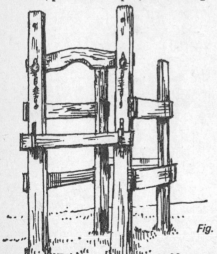

Fig. 22. Stocks for shoeing difficult horses.

end of the buffer. Meanwhile the new shoe has been prepared on the anvil and is ready for trying on, being held against the flat of the hoof for seating and measuring. This usually causes a great deal of smoke and odour but no pain, or even discomfort, to the horse.

If the shoe is a good fit it is nailed on with the aid of a small shoeing hammer. Nails are driven into the bottom outer rim of the hoof, through nail holes, starting at the front and working round the sides. Because hooves tend to slope inwards, the nail points protrude about halfway up the side of each hoof and these protruding ends are clinched off, gently hammered over and *rasped*. Most of the shoeing tools are kept in a large open box with a centre cross handle and they are removed only when needed for a particular job.

The local smith soon gets to know the horses in the district that are likely to be brought to his forge and keeps sets of shoes ready for each different type. A new horse, however, may need a set

Fig. 23. Rasping
a hoof before
shoeing.

specially made. For this, careful measurements of the foot have to be taken and recorded. The length of iron required for a new shoe is cut to the right length by means of a cold sett and sledge-hammer. When forged and sufficiently heated, it is shaped with a catshead hammer. The groove is made with a fullering hammer and the nail holes with a punch hammer or pritchell.

---

6. Clog-making

This woodland and coppice industry flourished until shortly before the Second World War. Even during the 1930s many men and women in the mills of the industrial North wore wooden-soled clogs rather than ordinary shoes or boots; they are still worn in some mills. They were worn to a lesser extent in Scotland, Wales and parts of rural England for work on the land. Clogs had many advantages over boots as they were hard wearing, and so less likely to need repairs. Essentially worn as part of working dress, they were also associated with festive occasions: the clog dancing of Lancashire was renowned throughout Britain, developing into modern tap dancing. Today they are still worn in heavy industry for foot protection and steadiness, especially in steel mills.

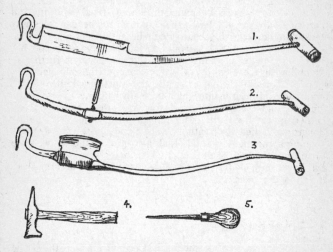

Fig. 24. Clog-making tools: 1. stock-knife; 2. morticing knife; 3. hollowing knife; 4. clogging hammer; 5. awl.

Whilst the continental sabot had wooden sides and uppers, the typical British clog had leather uppers, secured with straps or laces, and thick wooden soles made from a single strip of alder wood. They were often finished by a village craftsman, in his own shop and workshed. The man known as a 'clogger' found and prepared blocks of wood, working out of doors in field and woodland. The bulk manufacturer of clogs was usually supplied with most of his raw materials from outside sources and seldom cut wood or prepared leather himself.

The wood most commonly used was alder, but a useful alternative was sycamore, especially in parts of Wales. Both were comparatively easy to shape and yet had qualities of endurance. Neither wood was likely to split or chip under normal pressures and both were reasonably free of imperfections.

The clogger selected suitable trunks or branches, known as poles, which he then felled and stacked in heaps. The best for his purposes were between six and seven feet long and at least six inches in diameter. These poles were then sawn into lengths called *butts* by two men working a bow saw or crosscut saw between them.

The clogger shaped the rough blocks into clog soles with a stock knife — a long-handled knife with a stout blade, at the end of which was a hook. The hook was attached to a loop at the end of a narrow trestle astride which the clogger stood as he worked the knife with a levering action. With experience very precise work could be done with this tool and with similarly fixed hollowing and mortising knives used later by the clog-maker. The clog soles were stacked in the clogger's yard, made up in the form of a beehive for ventilation, so that the clogs would season and dry out thoroughly.

The clog-maker or manufacturer shaped the soles further — the hollowing knife cut into the upper part of the sole giving the shape essential for comfort, while the mortising knife cut the groove around the sole into which the leather uppers fitted — then trimmed and smoothed them. Iron soles were nailed on and leather uppers fixed, the latter pulled into position with lasting pincers and nailed down with a row of metal studs, using a special clogging hammer. As a final touch a strip of leather or welt was attached to the base of the uppers. Lace holes were made with an awl. Lancashire clogs usually had steel strips nailed across as well as round the soles.

7. Scythe-making

Before the invention of the mechanical reaping machine the scythe was one of the most important tools on the farm. At harvest time gangs of men would assemble to cut a field of hay or standing

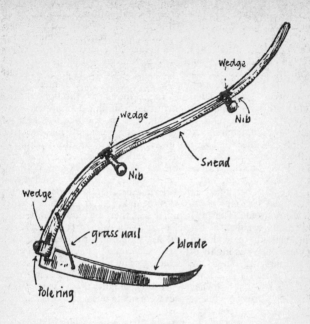

Fig. 25. Parts of a scythe.

corn, working from dawn to dusk. In later years the scythe was still useful and reserved for mowing in awkward places or to open a pathway for the machines. It could also be used, with great advantage, when crops had been flattened by storms.

The blades of scythes were often made in workshops or small factories, a number of which were rural industries based in villages. The most important centre of this craft, until recent years, was the Worcestershire village of Belbroughton, midway between Stourbridge and Bromsgrove, at the foot of the Clent Hills. In former times most scythes and cutting tools for country use were made by the local blacksmith, and there were few specialists before the 1790s. The trade of scythe-grinder, perhaps a man employed by a blacksmith, was recorded in Clent village, a short distance from Belbroughton, as early as 1520. Members of the Waldron family were making scythes in Clent and neighbouring hamlets as early as 1588, many of these being traded beyond the local areas.

At Bell End, on the outskirts of Belbroughton, there is said to have been a blade mill and forge of great antiquity, producing all kinds of cutting instruments from swords to scythes and billhooks. The blades were made by a process of repeated hammering, heating and doubling the metal, greatly improved by the addition of carbon and by what appear to have been — for those days — sophisticated techniques. The blade mill was eventually demolished to make way for a new road, but its methods of production long influenced local industry, throughout the eighteenth and nineteenth centuries. Similar techniques were employed at the Old Water Forge, in the main street of Belbroughton, from about 1750. This forge not only made scythes but plated other bladed instruments made by smiths working in Belbroughton, Clent, Stourbridge and Bromsgrove.

In 1790 the Old Water Forge was bought by Thomas Waldron of Clent, who came to settle in the village. He assembled a new plant using water-powered tilt hammers and grindstones that could deal with all the processes of making and finishing scythes on a large scale. The tilt hammer was then an innovation and its skilful use enabled the rate of production to be greatly increased. The methods of Waldron and his sons and brothers were soon acknowledged as highly efficient and copied in several centres as far apart as Sheffield, Dudley and Mells in Somerset. Belbroughton and a few other villages of north Worcestershire, however, remained the heart of this rural industry for many years. From the 1820s very few scythes were made by local blacksmiths in any part of the country.

There were several advantages that made Belbroughton an important centre for scythe-making, especially in the days of water power. The village was built on the banks of the Belne Brook, a swift-flowing stream descending from the Clent Hills, which fell about five hundred feet in four miles and seldom failed even during severe drought. During the middle ages there had been at least five corn mills working on the upper reaches of the brook, and these were later converted to scythe or blade mills. The ore for smelting was ready to hand in an area that later became known as the Black Country, north-east of Stourbridge. At first cold iron was imported from Stourbridge, but eventually a great quantity of both iron and iron ore came from the Forest of Dean via the River Severn, unloaded at the inland ports of Bewdley and later Stourport. It was transported in packhorse trains from the Severn landing places to forges in the Birmingham area, the route of these trains passing through a gap in the Clent Hills near Belbroughton, which became a place of rest and refreshment for the drivers. By the time cheaper ores had been introduced from Sweden and other continental countries, the industry was firmly established in the area. Coal was also necessary to feed the forges and furnaces, this being mined at Amblecote and Halesowen, only a few miles away and connected by good roads. Grindstones came from Alveley, near Bewdley, also in the nearby Severn valley.

Although the making of *sneads*, the curved wooden handles of the scythes, had long been a village craft in the west midlands, these, oddly, were imported wholesale, first from Scotland and later from the North American colonies, where craft skills were allied with highly efficient business methods. Even if the imported sneads were not always of the highest standard, they were good of their kind and commercially minded exporters could be depended upon to keep up their quota.

In time it was discovered that strengthening the scythe back was desirable and that this was better done using a metal entirely different from the edge. This led to the 'sandwich method', in which mild and blister steel were sandwiched between sections of Swedish iron. The sandwiches were first clamped down with the use of box tongs, then hammered and heated into a pair of strings. The strings were further beaten out, under a plating hammer, forming a *skelp* or raised edge to lie along the back of each blade. This was finally hammered down along the blade and planished to make it smooth and even.

Once the skelp was turned and fitted, the curved end of the blade was formed and the *crewe*, attaching the blade to the handle, was also fixed. The blade was then *trigged* or beaten cold under a power hammer and subjected to the final stages of tempering and grinding, which were always done by hand.

The monopoly of the Waldron family was challenged by a Worcestershire man named Isaac Nash during the 1840s. Nash was a yeoman farmer of Ombersley near Worcester, who also appeared to trade in iron products and to have invested in a plating mill at Dudley. He later gave up farming and bought a mill on the upper Belne, where he subcontracted to the Waldron firm and to firms in Cradley Heath. When the Waldrons failed in business, first through flooding and later through the loss of American contracts as a result of the Civil War, he was able to buy them out and establish himself at the Belbroughton plant in 1873. He soon set about buying up all the other blade and scythe mills, not only in the west midlands but also in other parts of the country, running them down to keep the orders in his own books. The industry continued at Belbroughton until the 1950s, still mainly in the hands of the Nash family. In later years, however, activity was confined to one mill where a number of modern devices had been installed. Electrically driven Bradley hammers were introduced in 1937, although the decline of water power began as early as the 1920s with the installation of a small gas engine.

Scythes are no longer made in Belbroughton but it is still possible to see the remains of mill dams, leats and early buildings or workshops associated with the craft. Deep and swift streams rushing down from the Clent Hills to join the Severn and Stour drove many small mills and powered village industries throughout north Worcestershire. Many of these may be traced back to even earlier than the Civil War.

Making scythe handles

The curious but strangely beautiful shape of the scythe handle or snead is unique among farm tools and implements. It is made, as a cottage craft, from young saplings with natural bends as near the right places as possible. After cutting and collection these are placed in a steam chest or oven for about thirty minutes to make them pliant and supple. They are then fixed in a special vice that resembles a ladder with close rungs, or they are positioned by supporting poles and wedges, which bend them even nearer to shape. At a later stage they are put in a setting frame for at least three days, ensuring full rigidity.

When they arrive at the craftsman's shop the saplings are slightly uneven and still covered with pieces of bark. The remaining bark is stripped off and the undersurface smoothed or polished. This is done with a smoothing engine or plane, a hand tool twisted round the entire length of the snead from top to bottom, before bending and setting. On leaving the setting frame the snead is further smoothed and finished with sandpaper.

The hand grips or *nibs* are added later and may be formed by hand but in more recent years have been turned out on a workshop lathe. Most nibs are made from withies. The blade and other metal parts were fitted and made by a blacksmith or scythe-grinder.

Fig. 26. Sneads in a setting frame or rack.

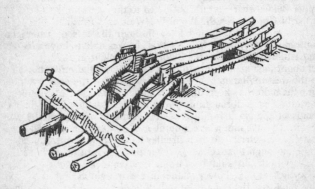

8. Coracles and coracle-making

Coracles are small keel-less boats of wickerwork, usually bowl-shaped. They were used mainly in country districts, especially in swift-flowing rivers and streams with rocks and rapids, or in fenland areas of the eastern counties. They were related to the skin-boat tradition of north-western Europe, flourishing among Celtic peoples from a very early period. In Britain they were used and made by both Britons and Saxons, surviving in large numbers on the rivers Wye, Dee and Severn and also in west Wales, until comparatively recent times. Some are still being made in Wales and the Severn Valley, especially at Ironbridge, Salop.

The coracle in Britain was closely akin to the larger Irish curragh, a sea-going and estuarine fishing vessel, also used round the coast of Dyfed during the third century AD. It was in such a craft that Irish or Welsh navigators may have visited North America long before Columbus, Cabot or even the Vikings. Such craft were eventually replaced by the clinker-built boat (with clinched, overlapping side planks) in coastal waters but survived on inland waterways, used by non-professional boatmen such as farmers, anglers and reed-cutters. In Wales and the Welsh Marches they were used mainly for salmon-netting on the rivers Towy, Teifi, Taff, Dee and Severn. This, however, was made illegal in some areas, ending on the Severn in 1936. Coracle racing on the Severn ended in 1926. Salmon-netting has continued longer in west Wales but only under strict supervision and limited conditions. As some licences expired they were allowed to lapse and new licences are no longer issued.

The great advantage of the coracle was its lightness and ease of construction. It was ideal for portage, being carried by means of a strap or cord attached to the centre-seat, either on the back or shoulder, leaving at least one hand free for nets and paddle. The coracle was seldom moored in the water or tied to the bank. It was normally stored in a barn, outhouse or even the farmhouse kitchen, propped against the wall in a near upright position.

Apart from salmon-netting and other fishing the coracle could be used for a variety of purposes from ferrying streams without bridges or fords to harvesting reeds (needed for thatching) and washing sheep in rivers.

Each coracle was constructed to suit local conditions and the needs of its owner. Perhaps the most familiar type was used on the Teifi in west Wales. This was semicircular aft of the cross-seat, with a flattish prow, the centre part or midships being narrower than the rest of the craft, slightly waisted. There was a slight bulge or overlap below the gunwale, and it lay deeper in the water than most coracles. It could thus withstand the dangerous rapids and sudden changes of level encountered in many Welsh streams.

37

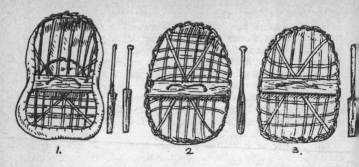

Fig. 27. Three main types of coracle: 1. Teifi; 2. Severn (Shrewsbury); 3. Wye.

The Towy coracle, used on fairly calm waters below Carmarthen, was much flatter than examples from further west. Although not waisted, it had a slightly flattened prow.

The Wye coracle, formerly constructed in villages along the bank of the river near Hereford, had straighter sides than the Towy boat and a very flat, almost square-ended prow.

There were four main types surviving on the upper reaches of the Severn, most of them to be seen until shortly after the First World War. Foremost among these was the oval or Ironbridge type, used between Bewdley and Shrewsbury for fishing and general purposes. Three smaller versions of this type were used for net fishing between Welshpool and Shrewsbury. There was also a subovate type, similar to the Wye craft, a near oval type used at Bridgnorth and a type with inward bent or tumblehome sides, also used on the Dee and Conway and in other parts of north Wales.

The ribs of the boat, which tended to resemble an open umbrella, were of ash or willow. The gunwale or upper line could be of withies or hazel rods and the outer covering of skins or rawhide. In later years, however, skins were often replaced by light canvas, flannel or calico tarred and made sufficiently waterproof. Laths for the framework were fashioned with a hoop shaver, as used by coopers or barrel-makers.

The various parts were first woven together, as in basketry. Next the cross-seat (an ordinary plank) with its carrying loop was inserted and the cover pulled over, in the same way as a glove is drawn on to a hand. Covering was always done with the framework up-ended. The final stage was to fix the woven outer rim of the gunwale, slightly above seat level, but this was not fitted to all types.

The laths of the framework varied in number according to

locality. Those on the Teifi had nine across and six lengthways, while those at Ironbridge had eight each way. Other Severn coracles had seven each way, but these were set fairly wide apart and were much stouter in themselves. Most types had two extra laths or diagonals in the form of a St Andrew's cross. Nails were rarely used with the woven framework, and this improved the resilience and navigable qualities of the craft. An upper line or gunwale, however, could be nailed to the upturned ends of the laths, above water level. Very few hand tools were needed in construction, apart from a sharp-bladed instrument to cut and cleave the withies or hazel rods. A trestle or horse with a simple

Fig. 28. Coracle fisherman.

vice might be used for the shaving, the craftsman sitting astride and shaving towards the body, as in making trug baskets.

The Teifi coracle was between seventy-two and sixty-two inches in length, with a forty-inch beam at the bow or prow end, and thirty-four inches across the centre seat. Depth varied between twelve and seventeen inches. Average weight of most types was about thirty pounds. The Severn coracle was often slightly smaller and seldom more than sixty-five inches long and forty-seven inches wide, with a depth of fourteen inches.

A coracle would have a cross loop or strap fixed to the seat; this was sometimes a broad leather band but more often a length of cord. Leather bands or straps were found mainly on the Severn below Shrewsbury.

Paddles were about five feet long, consisting of blade, loom and crutch (end, middle and cross handle).

Large and small mesh fishing nets were used, made of hemp, with strong horsehair ropes for hauling in. Most fishermen had a small baton or fish club for stunning salmon as they were taken from the nets. These were known as *priests* and made of boxwood, about fourteen inches long. When not in use the priest was kept in the prow or under the seat.

Coracles may be seen in several museums including the Welsh Folk Museum at St Fagans near Cardiff, the Museum of English Rural Life at Reading and the Hereford and Worcester County Museum at Hartlebury near Kidderminster. They are still in use on certain Welsh rivers and during Cilgerran Festival Week, on the third Saturday in August, there are aquatic displays and races between coracles, with both open events and special classes. Coracles are still made and used by Mr E. Rogers on the banks of the Severn at Ironbridge. Although net fishing is now restricted there are signs that coracles may return to favour for fly fishing, being lighter for portage and much handier than a wooden boat.

One paddle only is used, plied from the centre of the boat. On all types of coracle the flat end is the prow or bows and the rounder end the stern, where there is a marked difference. The paddle is used two-handed for propulsion, with a strong figure of eight movement, but single-handed to keep the boat steady. In salmon-netting the nets are trawled between two boats of the same size. One hand is used for holding the net and the other to hold the paddle.

9. Dry walling

In parts of western and northern Britain, including the mountains of Wales, much of Scotland, the Pennines, Cornwall and the Lake District, where stone is plentiful and there may be insufficient wood to make fences, dry stone walls are found, providing excellent protection against rough weather, sheltering livestock and preventing top soil from blowing away. The majority date from eighteenth-century land enclosures.

In the Cotswold uplands there are both stone walls and hedges and it is in this area that some of the finest traditions of walling and hedging are still preserved.

Stone walling in Britain may be the work of specialists known as dykers or wallers, or sometimes of local masons usually employed in building stone cottages and barns. On some holdings the farmer or his men have the skill to rebuild or at least repair their own walls, which, with a little attention, may last for several generations and outlast a number of wooden fences. A skilled man can lay about six yards of double wall in a working day.

According to tradition there should be no mortar or cement binding the blocks of a dry-stone wall together. In modern practice, the waller sometimes uses a binding of lime and sand mortar to hold the top, capping or coping stones in place; this increases stability, improves overall appearance and is flexible enough to move with the wall over the years.

A wall over four feet high is really two interlinked walls with solid pieces of filling where necessary and flat, wide tie or through stones the full width of the wall at regular intervals. In all cases the wall is of irregular stonework, no two pieces being exactly alike, although there is greater uniformity among the capping stones than in the body of the wall. The required number of selected sizes of stones is spread out along the length of the wall to be constructed. Large stones form a foundation usually based on wooden templates set at intervals and connected by guide strings. As the courses are laid larger stones give way to smaller ones so that the wall slopes towards the top, giving it a batter or inclination. The outer edge of the stone should slope slightly downwards to shed water so the inner edge must be carefully pinned to secure its position.

Pennine and north country walls or dykes may be of either double or single thickness.

Walls between farms or estates and bordering highways are usually of double thickness, more substantial than those dividing fields and enclosures on the same property. The double walls are upwards of four feet six inches high, sometimes very much higher, according to local needs. The inner boundary walls of single thickness are merely up to four feet high.

In parts of Scotland there are stone walls known as Galloway dykes which have a partly double and partly single thickness, being forty inches at the base and twenty inches on top. Many walls of this type are known to have remained intact since the mid eighteenth century.

Fig. 29. Repairing a stone wall.

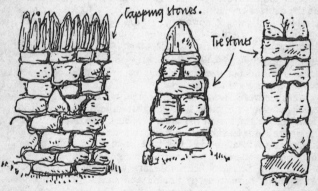

Fig. 30. Dry-stone walling: (left) side elevation; (centre) end elevation; (right) plan of cross-section.

42

Outer boundary walls in the Cotswolds are sometimes of considerable height, especially when enclosing a private estate, but those between fields on the same property are seldom more than three feet high. The stones from which they are made are more regular than those of the Pennines and appear as smaller, neater blocks. Each wall is twenty inches thick at the base, decreasing to fifteen or sixteen inches at the coping line. The slightly irregular capping stones are known in this area as *combers*. Large stones built into the thickness or heart of the wall, several inches deep, tend to slope outwards to drain off rain and snow. Most walls are of single thickness. The colour of stone walls, especially in Cotswold areas, varies from a strong amber to a mild or dull grey.

A dry waller needs very few tools. These include a mason's hammer of about four pounds weight, a small pick and a pair of protective leather pads to cover the palms of his hands.

10. Hedging

The hedges that enclose the smaller and medium-sized fields of the lowland areas are the equivalents of dry walls on higher ground. They are perhaps at their best and most useful for stock or mixed farming; like walls they offer protection and shelter for livestock. Arable farmers, however, tend to see them as places of refuge for birds and other pests, while they occupy cultivable land.

The main work of the hedger is to trim, lay and cultivate farm hedges and to clear up banks and clean out ditches. The job requires skill and some farmers prefer to grub out their hedges, on the grounds that their upkeep is no longer economical because of the high cost of labour and the shortage of properly trained manpower. While many farmworkers may be able to trim a hedge, there are fewer who understand the art of hedge-laying.

Maintenance of a recently laid hedge simply involves trimming and clearing out unwanted plants. Where the hedge has run wild the hedger starts by clearing the undergrowth and cutting back the side growth to the required width with upward strokes of the slasher. As he works along the hedge, usually from left to right, he leaves the young trees which will form the laid hedge — elm, hazel, oak, beech, ash and hornbeam.

After all branching stuff is cleared from the sapling the stem is cut halfway through, near the base, and bent over to the left at an angle of sixty degrees or more. (There must be enough uncut stem to allow the sap to rise and keep the tree alive and encourage the branches to tiller out, particularly at the bottom.) As each stem or *stool* is bent over, the way is cleared for the next one to lie beside, overlapping it, often to a length of ten feet or more. At intervals of about two feet, vertical stakes or *stabbers* are driven

43

into the ground and the stools are woven around them as work progresses. Suitable upright saplings may be used as stakes, trimmed to hedge height later on. The whole mesh is knocked in and tightened with the hammer or *bitel*.

Finally the top of the hedge is bound by intertwining slender rods or runners in and out of the stabbers and stools. The long runners of bramble, elm or hazel, tall thin saplings left for the purpose and bent at right angles or specially cut hazel rods are used, several twisted together forming a continuous, flexible cable link along the top.

A good craftsman makes sure his hedges are as firm and even as possible, with limbs bent fairly near the ground. Weaker parts are interwoven with elm or hazel rods, called binders, which serve to form hurdles and give the hedge a finished appearance. The aim is to prolong the natural life of the hedge and to maintain it both as a cattle shelter and barrier. While the hedge should not be too bushy and untidy on top it is also necessary to limit the size of lower or knotted growth at the base. Heathers or infilling materials growing between the stabbers should be bent upwards, all pointing in much the same direction.

Fig. 31. A hedger at work.

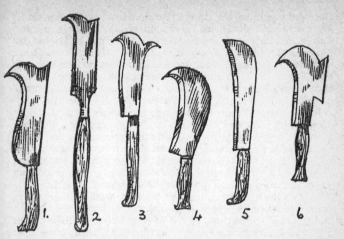

Fig. 32. A selection of billhooks used for hedging: 1. from Norfolk; 2. and 3. from Yorkshire; 4. from Kent; 5. from Herefordshire; 6. from Nottinghamshire.

Trimming may be done at any time of the year but is mainly a winter task, often left until there is a slack period.

Tools and equipment used by hedgers include protective gloves, the bitel, and long-handled and small slashing hooks, which vary in design throughout England and Wales. A traditional hedger often wears his trousers hitched up below his knees, a battered cap or hat and — in wet weather — an empty oat sack round his shoulders.

11. Hurdle-making

Hurdles are useful items about the farm and serve to mend gaps in hedges, to fold or pen sheep and smaller livestock, and to limit grazing as temporary fencing. Perhaps the best-known type is the bar hurdle, which is cleft from ash or hazel and resembles a small gate without posts or hinges. The second type is almost the same size as the first but is made of withies or hazel twigs woven into a sturdy framework of hazel or ash poles.

In the old days hurdle-makers often lived near their work, for weeks on end, in huts or shelters. These provided a place to keep their tools and cover under which to work on wet days. On the sheltered side of each hut would be stored two or three posts or logs of regular shape and thickness, about the length of the hurdle, and known as *moulds*. One of these would be laid on the ground and held in position by pegs or wedges. The rods to be used in making the hurdles are trimmed and cut to length on a chopping block. Then a small razor-keen billhook is used to split each rod from top to bottom. Stakes about four feet long, known as *sails*, form the uprights of the hurdles.

Nine or ten sails are inserted into corresponding holes in the mould, with a thicker rod at each end for extra strength. Rods are then interwoven horizontally between the uprights, starting at the bottom with what are known as *spurs*, long thin rods, and ending with *finishers*. The twist of the rod at each end is particularly important: the hazel must not bend back on itself without twisting or it will break. Most good hurdle-makers keep their work, especially the weaving, as neat as possible, working the rods so that the split side appears on one side of the hurdle only. About two thirds of the way up the side of each hurdle are two twisted rods or *twillies*. These are worked round each other and interwoven with the uprights, forming a small aperture. This is known as the *twilly hole* and is used when carrying the hurdle from place to place; several hurdles can be hoisted on to a stake supported by a man's shoulder. About five heathers or small rods are woven above the twilly hole to strengthen and protect the edges. The weaving is finished and pushed tightly down; the woven area is about three feet deep.

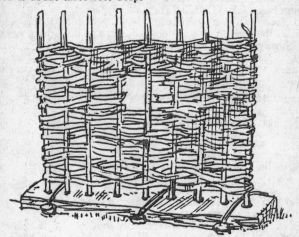

Fig. 33. Wattle hurdle on a mould.

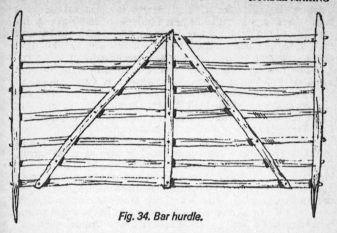

Fig. 34. Bar hurdle.

Rough and unsightly parts of the hurdle are trimmed with the billhook or round-headed axe, used in conjunction with a cudgel. The cudgel is also used to protect the parts to be trimmed, acting as a barrier tool. The end uprights are sharpened so that they will go into the ground easily. Working from the crack of dawn, the wattle hurdlemaker could weave about twelve hurdles per day. Although sometimes employed on a large estate, he was usually an independent craftsman paid so much for a dozen of his finished products.

The typical bar hurdle, which is preferred in some parts of the country, is often easier to handle, although not offering such complete protection. It is ideal for penning sheep and pigs, especially at a show, sale or open market. It usually has two uprights, six or seven crossbars, a vertical centre bar, and two diagonal brace bars. These are cleft rather than saw-cut from ashwood, withy or hazel — as cleft bars prove much stronger than sawn ones. The uprights, known as heads, are mortised to take the crossbars and are sharply carved or pointed at one end for driving into the ground. When the crossbars are fixed, the diagonal bracebars and the centre bar are nailed on with cut nails. Sheep hurdles are six feet long and three feet six inches high.

12. Charcoal-burning

Charcoal has had many uses, perhaps the most important of which were connected with the early smelting of iron ore. It was used in the manufacture of gunpowder, the fusion of glassmaking ingredients, for filters, and in making sticks of charcoal for drawing. The primitive metalworkers of the iron age prized it above other fuels for its great heat and lack of smoke as it burns with a small but intense flame. It was used in most countries until the discovery of coke and used widely in metal production until alternative methods of ore smelting were introduced.

The iron-smelting industry, once centred in what are now rural parts of Sussex and the south-eastern counties, supported large numbers of charcoal-burners, working in the woodland areas that covered most of the high Weald. These craftsmen were also found in many other forest areas, notably in the New Forest and the Wyre Forest.

The best woods for charcoal were alder, buckthorn, oak and chestnut, all timbers at one time found in most woodland areas.

In the course of preparation the wood had to be heated to a high temperature, but with insufficient air to cause full burning or open combustion. It was practical to make the charcoal in or near the woods, especially as there were few good roads in the forests.

After the wood had been gathered it was left to dry or season for a number of weeks, sometimes several months, depending on conditions. A circular area was then prepared in a clearing or on waste ground, and the stack was built in the centre. First a chimney of split logs was formed round a stake six feet high. Wood to be charred was piled round the centre, sloping to the top, eventually forming a domed or beehive *clamp*. The dome was thickly covered with clods, straw and turf, then with another layer of wood and finally with a covering of dirt and leaves about five inches thick. In this way air was almost entirely shut out from the centre. When finished, with its final layer of leaves and earth, the dome was fifteen to thirty feet across and upwards of five feet high.

Fig. 35. Charcoal-burner's mound.

When the mound was ready for burning, after allowing a short time to settle, the centre stake was withdrawn through the top and burning charcoal was dropped down the chimney. This was followed by a few dry sticks and then the chimney was sealed up, causing the fire to spread in an outward rather than an upward direction. This was known as *charring* and the process continued for at least ten days. During this time the charcoal burner was on watch at all hours, eating and sleeping near his work.

A short time after ignition the mound emitted a great deal of white but thickly clouded smoke, mainly moisture from the wood, then a thin blue haze of other elements. At last the haze died away and after a short period of final clearing, the outer covers of the dome were removed. Only a skilled burner, from long experience, could sense when the mound was ready to open. Great care had to be taken, to avoid damaging the charcoal or causing a flare-up, if the dome were opened too quickly or in the wrong way. After the charcoal had cooled down it was packed, ready for the customer, in sacks and containers.

There are now very few old-style charcoal-burners: charcoal is made nowadays by distillation, in which the former waste products like wood alcohol and tar are recovered, although in some parts kilns are used for more conventional burning. Like many other coppice and woodland workers the charcoal-burner was by nature and force of circumstances a solitary figure, mixing only with his own kind. During the season, which lasted for most of the summer, he seldom moved very far from his mound or dome. During the ten or more days of each charring the dome had to be dressed or recovered and a watch kept for fire breaks and uneven burning. It is not surprising that charcoal-burning was often a family occupation involving sons, uncles and brothers of two or three generations.

13. Museums

This chapter lists and gives basic information about museums in the British Isles where craft tools and the products of craftsmen may be seen. This information, particularly opening times, is liable to alteration and readers are advised to telephone a museum before making a special journey there.

ENGLAND

AVON

Blaise Castle House Museum
Henbury, Bristol (telephone: Bristol 625378)
Items of folk and craft interest. Open in afternoons daily throughout the year.

Castle Farm Folk Museum
Marshfield, near Chippenham, Wiltshire (telephone: Marshfield 469)

Collection of hand tools displayed in old farm buildings. Demonstrations of crafts, including basket-making, whenever possible. June to September, Wednesday, Saturday and Sunday afternoons.

BEDFORDSHIRE
Luton Museum and Art Gallery
Wardown Park, Luton (telephone: Luton 36941 or 36942)

Tools and items for crafts and local agriculture and industry. Weekdays 10 a.m. to 6 p.m., Sunday 2 p.m. to 6 p.m. (closing at 5 p.m. from October to March). Closed Christmas Day, Boxing Day, New Year's Day and Sundays in December and January.

BERKSHIRE
Courage Shire Horse Centre
Cherry Garden Lane, Maidenhead Thicket (telephone: Littlewick Green 3917)

Display of harness; farrier's shop. March to October, daily except non-holiday Mondays 11 a.m. to 4 p.m.

Museum of English Rural Life
University of Reading, Whiteknights Park, Reading (telephone: Reading 85123 extension 475)

Craft tools and documentary material. Papers and documents may be consulted on application to the Keeper. Tuesday to Saturday 10 a.m. to 1 p.m., 2 to 4.30 p.m. Closed Sunday, Monday and bank holidays.

BUCKINGHAMSHIRE
Buckinghamshire County Museum
Church Street, Aylesbury (telephone: Aylesbury 82158 or 88849)

New rural life gallery with craft tools and bygones. Monday to Friday, 9.30 a.m. to 5 p.m., Saturday 9.30 a.m. to 12.30 p.m. and 1.30 to 5 p.m.

CAMBRIDGESHIRE
Cambridge and County Folk Museum
2 and 3 Castle Street, Cambridge (telephone: Cambridge 55159)

Craft and agricultural tools. Open Tuesdays to Saturdays and on Sunday afternoons.

Farmland Museum
50 High Street, Haddenham, Ely (telephone: Haddenham 381)

Country craft and farm tools. First Sunday in each month until dusk.

CORNWALL

Helston Borough Museum
Old Butter Market, Helston
   Saddler's tools. Weekdays (except Wednesday) 10.30 a.m. to
12.30 p.m., 2 to 4.30 p.m. Wednesday 10.30 a.m. to 12.30 p.m.

North Cornwall Museum and Gallery
The Clease, Camelford
   Life in Cornwall in the late nineteenth century. Wagons and
hand tools. Daily, April to September.

CUMBRIA

Abbot Hall Museum of Lakeland Life and Industry
Kendal (telephone: Kendal 22464)
   Tools and materials relating to local crafts. Monday to
Friday, 10.30 a.m. to 12.30 p.m. and 2 to 5 p.m. Saturday and
Sunday 2 to 5 p.m. Closed over Christmas and New Year and on
Good Friday.

DERBYSHIRE

Elvaston Castle
Borrowash Road, Elvaston (telephone: Derby 71342)
   Displays of rural craft workshops and horse-drawn vehicles.
Open all year round.

The Old House Museum
Cunningham Place, Bakewell (telephone: Bakewell 2378)
   Craft tools and implements. Easter to the end of September,
daily 2.30 to 5 p.m.

DEVON

Ashley Countryside Collection
Winkleigh (telephone: Ashreigney 226)
   Many craftsmen's tools. Open Easter to mid September on
Wednesdays, Saturdays, Sundays and public holidays (in August
daily except Thursdays).

James Countryside Museum
Bicton Gardens, East Budleigh (telephone: Budleigh Salterton
3881)
   Rural implements and craft tools. Open from late March to
October 12 to 6 p.m. (Easter weekend 11 a.m. to 6 p.m.).

Steam and Countryside Museum
 Sandy Bay, Exmouth
   Country craft tools, including those of the blacksmith and
wheelwright. Open daily from May to October.

Tiverton Museum
St Andrew's Street, Tiverton (telephone: Tiverton 56295)
   Wagons and carts. Open daily except bank holidays and Christmas week.

DORSET
Brewery Farm Museum
Milton Abbas
   Tools connected with farming and rural crafts. Open daylight hours, every day throughout the year.

Dorset County Museum
Dorchester (telephone: Dorchester 2735)
Rural crafts collection. Open daily except Sundays.

DURHAM
North of England Open Air Museum
Beamish Hall, Beamish, Stanley (telephone: Stanley 33580 and 33586)
   Craft tools and items. Craftsmen frequently at work. Open daily from June to August. From Easter to end of May and in September open daily except Mondays. October to Easter: reduced hours of opening.

EAST SUSSEX
Brighton Museum and Art Gallery
Church Street, Brighton (telephone: Brighton 63005)
   Local crafts and craft tools. Folk interest connected with East: Sussex. Open Tuesdays to Saturdays, and Sunday afternoons.

GLOUCESTERSHIRE
Bishop Hooper's Lodging
99 - 103 Westgate Street, Gloucester (telephone: Gloucester 24131)
   Items relating to crafts and agriculture. Weekdays 10 a.m. to 5.30 p.m.

Smerrill Farm Museum
Near Kemble, Cirencester
   Craft and farm tools displayed in a delightful Cotswold barn. Open daily.

GREATER LONDON
Upminster Tithe Barn Agricultural and Folk Museum
Hall Lane, Upminster (telephone enquiries: Upminster 29614)

Exhibits relating to rural crafts, and much else, in a fifteenth-century barn. April to October, first weekend in each month, 11 a.m. to 1 p.m. and 2.15 to 5.30 p.m.

HAMPSHIRE
Breamore Countryside Museum
Breamore House, Breamore (telephone: Breamore 468)
Wheelwright's shop and forge. April to September daily except non-holiday Mondays and Fridays, 2 to 5.30 p.m.

Curtis Museum
High Street, Alton (telephone: Alton 82802)
Local craft tools. Open daily except Sundays and bank holidays.

HEREFORD AND WORCESTER
Almonry Museum
Vine Street, Evesham (telephone: Evesham 6944)
Craft tools and agricultural implements. Open March to September, each afternoon except Mondays and Wednesdays.

Bewdley Museum
The Shambles, Load Street, Bewdley (telephone: Bewdley 403573)
Craft tools of local interest. Material and display relating to charcoal-burning. Open March to November, Mondays to Saturdays and Sunday afternoons.

Country Centre
Clows Top, near Bewdley (telephone: Clows Top 358)
Displays of saddler's, wheelwright's and blacksmith's shops. Sundays and bank holidays, Easter to the end of September, 10.30 a.m. to 7 p.m.

Hereford and Worcester County Museum
Hartlebury Castle, Hartlebury, near Kidderminster (telephone: Hartlebury 416)
Craft tools, smith's forge, wheelwright's shop. Open February to November, Monday to Thursday and also Saturday and Sunday afternoons.

HERTFORDSHIRE
Ashwell Village Museum
Swan Street, Ashwell, near Baldock
Items illustrating country and village life from prehistoric to contemporary times. Sundays 3 to 5.30 p.m. or by appointment (write to the Curator for appointments).

St Albans City Museum
Hatfield Road, St Albans (telephone: St Albans 56679)
Country craft tools and implements. Blacksmith's shop and
wheelwright's shop. Weekdays 10 a.m. to 5 p.m.

LANCASHIRE
Towneley Hall Art Gallery and Museum
Burnley (telephone: Burnley 24213)
Museum of Local Crafts and Industries. Craft tools and.
bygones. Open Monday to Friday, and also Sunday afternoons.

LEICESTERSHIRE
Rutland County Museum
Catmos Street, Oakham (telephone: Oakham 3654)
Craft tools and agricultural implements. Tuesday to Saturday
10 a.m. to 1 p.m. and 2 to 5 p.m. Sundays (April to October) 2 to 5
p.m. Closed Christmas Day, Boxing Day and Good Friday.

LINCOLNSHIRE
Church Farm Museum
Church Road South, Skegness (telephone: Skegness 66658)
Workshop displays illustrating the work of the blacksmith,
farrier and saddler. Open April to September, daily.

Museum of Lincolnshire Life
Burton Road, Lincoln (telephone: Lincoln 28448)
Craft items relating to the work of the blacksmith, wheelwright
and saddler. Open Monday to Saturday, and Sunday afternoons.

NORFOLK
Bridewell Museum of Local Industries
Bridewell Alley, Norwich (telephone: Norwich 22233)
Craft tools. Weekdays 10 a.m. to 5 p.m.

NORTHAMPTONSHIRE
Museum of Leathercraft
Old Blue Coat School, Bridge Street, Northampton (telephone:
Northampton 34881)
Items connected with harness-making and saddlery. Open
Mondays to Saturdays.

NORTH YORKSHIRE
Ryedale Folk Museum
Hutton-le-Hole (telephone: Lastingham 367)
Craft tools and blacksmith's forge. Open in afternoons from
Easter to end of September.

York Castle Museum
Tower Street, York (telephone: York 53611)
Craft tools and agricultural bygones. Open daily.

OXFORDSHIRE
Cotswold Folk and Agricultural Museum
c/o Andrews Cottage, Asthall Barrow, Burford (telephone: Burford 2178)
Depicts Cotswold rural life in the nineteenth century and includes a saddler's shop. May to October, first and third Sunday of each month, 2 to 5 p.m.

Oxfordshire County Museum
Fletcher's House, Woodstock (telephone: Woodstock 811456)
Craft tools. Open Monday to Saturday, and on Sunday afternoons, but closed Mondays from October to April.

SALOP
Acton Scott Working Farm Museum
Wenlock Edge, Acton Scott, near Church Stretton (telephone: Marshbrook 306/307)
Traditional crafts are demonstrated at weekends.

The White House Museum of Buildings and Country Life
Munslow Aston
Craft tools and farm implements. Open Saturday and Wednesday afternoons from April to October, and Tuesdays and Thursdays also from June to August.

SOMERSET
The Ingram-Fowler Country Life Museum
Cricket St Thomas Wildlife Park, near Chard
Over a thousand items of rural and agricultural interest, including many hand tools.

Somerset Rural Life Museum
Abbey Barn, Glastonbury (telephone enquiries: Taunton 3451 extension 374)
Rural craft displays relating especially to Somerset, such as the withy industry. Open Monday to Saturday and Sunday afternoons.

SOUTH YORKSHIRE
Abbeydale Industrial Hamlet
Abbeydale Road South, Sheffield 7 (telephone: Sheffield 367731)
Hand forges, craft tools and a scythe works. Weekdays 10 a.m. to 5 p.m., Sundays 11 a.m. to 5 p.m. (Spring Bank Holiday to Summer Bank Holiday: weekdays 10 a.m. to 8 p.m., Sundays 11 a.m. to 8 p.m.).

STAFFORDSHIRE

Staffordshire County Museum and Mansion House

Shugborough, near Stafford (telephone: Little Haywood 388)

Craft tools and implements. Open Tuesday to Friday throughout the year, also Saturday and Sunday afternoons from mid March to mid October and first and third Sunday afternoons in each month from mid October to mid March.

SUFFOLK

Easton Farm Park

Model Farm, Easton, Woodbridge (telephone: Wickham Market 746475)

Hand tools and demonstrations of local crafts. Good Friday to first Sunday in October, Wednesday to Sunday and bank holidays, 10.30 a.m. to 6 p.m.

Museum of East Anglian Life

Abbots Hall, Stowmarket (telephone: Stowmarket 2229)

Amongst the reconstructed buildings is a blacksmith's forge. Rural crafts. April to October, weekdays 11 a.m. to 5 p.m., Sunday 2 to 5 p.m.

Sicklesmere Forge

Sicklesmere, near Bury St Edmunds. Owned by Mrs Genevieve Bedford, Pond Ley, Cocks Green, Great Welnetham, Bury St Edmunds.

Though the forge is now a shop selling bygones the displays of wheelwright's and blacksmith's tools are permanent and the furnace can still be used.

SURREY

Old Kiln Museum

Reeds Road, Tilford, Farnham (telephone: Frensham 2300)

A blacksmith's and wheelwright's shop, and many other items. Open March to September, Wednesdays, Saturdays, Sundays and bank holidays.

WARWICKSHIRE

Mary Arden's House

Wilmcote (telephone: Stratford-upon-Avon 3455)

Blacksmith's and wheelwright's tools. April to October, weekdays 9 a.m. to 6 p.m. November to March, weekdays, 9 a.m. to 12.45 p.m. and 2 to 4 p.m.

Museum of Country Bygones
The Orchard, High Street, Marton (telephone: Leamington Spa 27030, between 9.30 a.m. and 4.30 p.m.).
The tools of blacksmiths, wheelwrights and thatchers. Open weekends and bank holidays, Easter Monday to October, 10 a.m. to 8 p.m.

WEST SUSSEX
Horsham Museum
Causeway House, The Causeway, Horsham (telephone: Horsham 4959)
Tools relating to crafts in West Sussex. Blacksmith's forge, saddler's shop and wheelwright's workshop equipment. Open Tuesday to Friday afternoons and Saturdays.

Weald and Downland Open Air Museum
Singleton, near Chichester (telephone: Singleton 348)
Exhibits include a forge, wheelwright's tools and a charcoal-burner's hut. Open April to September daily except Mondays (but open bank holidays and Mondays in August); in October on Wednesdays, Saturdays and Sundays; November to March, Sundays only.

WEST YORKSHIRE
Abbey House Museum
Kirkstall, Leeds (telephone: Leeds 55821)
Craft tools and workshops. April to September, weekdays 10 a.m. to 6 p.m., Sunday 2 to 6 p.m. October to March, weekdays 10 a.m. to 5 p.m., Sunday 2 to 5 p.m.

Cliffe Castle Art Gallery and Museum
Keighley (telephone: Keighley 64184)
Craft tools and demonstrations in reconstructed workshops. Open daily.

Colne Valley Museum
Cliffe Ash, Golcar, Huddersfield (telephone: Huddersfield 59762)
A clog-maker's shop. Also craft tools and items of folk-craft interest. Saturdays and Sundays throughout the year (also bank holidays).

Heptonstall Old Grammar School Museum
Heptonstall, near Hebden Bridge (telephone enquiries: Elland 2540)
Craft workshops, tools and agricultural items. Open Saturdays, Sundays and public holidays in afternoon.

Pennine Farm Museum
Ripponden, near Halifax (telephone enquiries: Elland 2540)
Agricultural and craft tools. Easter to September, Saturday, Sunday and public holidays, 2 to 5 p.m.

West Yorkshire Folk Museum
Shibden Hall, Shibden Park, Halifax (telephone: Halifax 52246).
Craft tools, implements and workshops. Open Mondays to Saturdays from March to November, and Sunday afternoons from February to November.

WILTSHIRE
Salisbury and South Wiltshire Museum
St Ann Street, Salisbury.
Craft tools. Open Mondays to Saturdays throughout the year, and Sunday afternoons in July and August.

ISLE OF MAN

Manx Village Folk Museum
Cregneash (telephone: Douglas 5522)
Craft tools and blacksmith's shop. Open mid May to late September, Mondays to Saturdays, and Sunday afternoons.

SCOTLAND
DUMFRIES AND GALLOWAY
Dumfries Museum
The Observatory, Corberry Hill, Dumfries (telephone: Dumfries 3374)
Craft tools and folk life. Open Mondays, Wednesdays to Saturdays, and Sunday afternoons, but closed on Sundays from October to March.

HIGHLAND
Highland Folk Museum
Duke Street, Kingussie, Inverness-shire (telephone: Kingussie 307)
Craft tools. Open Mondays to Saturdays throughout the year, and also Sunday afternoons from April to October.

LOTHIAN
National Museum of Antiquities of Scotland
Queen Street, Edinburgh 2 (telephone: 031-556 8921)
Agricultural and crafts section. Weekdays 10 a.m. to 5 p.m., Sunday 2 to 5 p.m.

STRATHCLYDE
Gladstone Court
Biggar, Lanarkshire (telephone: Biggar 20005)
Workshops and craft tools. Easter to October, daily 10 a.m..
to 12.30 p.m. and 2 to 5 p.m. Closed Sunday mornings and local
holidays.

TAYSIDE
Angus Folk Museum
Kirkwynd Cottages, Glamis, Angus
Craft tools and agricultural implements. Daily from May to
September, 1 to 6 p.m.

Glenesk Museum
The Retreat, Glenesk, Angus (telephone: Tarfside 236)
Tools of local crafts and agricultural implements. Sundays
from Easter and daily from 1st June to 30th September.

WALES
GWENT
Abergavenny and District Museum
Castle House, Castle Street, Abergavenny (telephone:
Abergavenny 4282)
A saddler's shop and craft tools. Weekdays 11 a.m. to 1 p.m.
and 2 to 5 p.m., Sundays 2 to 5 p.m. Closed Wednesday and
Sunday, November to March.

Rural Crafts Museum
Llanvapley, Abergavenny (telephone: Llantilio 210)
Tools and equipment used in thatching, blacksmithing,
etc. Sundays 3 to 6 p.m. or until dusk.

SOUTH GLAMORGAN
Welsh Folk Museum
St Fagans, Cardiff (telephone: Cardiff 561357)
Craft tools and items of folk interest. Open Mondays to
Saturdays and Sunday afternoons. Closed on May Day, Christmas
Eve, Christmas Day, Boxing Day and New Year's Day.

NORTHERN IRELAND
Ulster Folk and Transport Museum
Cultra Manor, Holywood, County Down (telephone: Holywood
5411)

Blacksmith's forge, craft tools and bygones. Open Mondays to Saturdays, and on Sunday afternoons.

REPUBLIC OF IRELAND
National Museum of Ireland
Kildare Street, Dublin (telephone: Dublin 765521)
Craft tools and items concerning folk life. Tuesday to Saturday, 10 a.m. to 5 p.m. Sunday 2 to 5 p.m.

Glossary of tools and craft terms

Auger: Boring tool with a cross handle at the top, used in many country crafts.
Bitel, bittell or beetle: A barrel-headed mallet, often fitted with two metal rings, one at each end of the head.
Blinkers: The eye pieces on a draught bridle.
Body: The leather outer side of a horse's collar.
Bond: Iron tie on a wagon wheel; also a band round a wheelstock.
Bond twister: An iron crank used to extract lengths of straw from a rick in thatching.
Boxing engine: A device with a three-pronged cutter used by the wheelwright to cut the large hole made through the elm wheel hub.
Breeze: Small coal used by a smith in his hearth.
Buffer: Double-ended chisel employed in horse-shoeing.
Buzz: A scraper with an upright blade, used as a spokeshave.
Cantle: The high rounded part at the rear of a saddle.
Charring: The firing process in making charcoal.
Cleft wood: A stake of wood, cleft for use by a craftsman.
Clinch: The hammering over of the nail-ends which protrude through a horse's hoof in the process of shoeing.
Combers: Capping stones used in dry walling.
Compass race: A form of compasses used for marking out grooves in leather.
Cord: A pile or bundle of newly cut branches.
Creasing iron: Tool for making the indentations in harness straps, etc.
Crupper: Short backstraps through which the horse's tail is looped in harness.
Dags: Small nails or spikes used to fix iron bands round the head of a mallet or bitel.
Draw down: Hammer out metal to make it thinner.
Felloes: The outer segments of the wheel.
Finishers: The final rods which are used to finish off the top of a wattle hurdle.

F wrench: Tool shaped like a letter F, used in twisting metal.

Gullet: The fore part of the tree in saddle-making.

Half-moon knife: A knife used in leather and harness work with a semicircular blade.

Hames: Metal bars fixed in grooves either side of a horse's collar.

Helm: One of the many bundles of straw selected for thatching.

Hollowing knife: A type of stock-knife used in clog-making, for hollowing the sole of the rough clog to fit the contours of the foot.

Jarvis: A rounded shave for rounding the spokes, used by wheelwrights.

Leasing: Bundles of thatching straw.

Leggat: A small spade-like bat used to beat down the reeds when thatching a roof.

Martingale: A leather strap attached to the lower part of a horse's neck collar.

Mortising knife: A type of stock-knife used in clog-making to cut the groove around the sole to take the leather upper.

Mould: The log or frame in which a wattle hurdle is made.

Nave: The wheelstock or hub.

Opening tool: An iron arm-sheath like a pointed scoop used in reed thatching.

Palm iron: A protective thimble worn on the palm in harness-making.

Plough-gauge: Tool used to cut straight leather straps or rolls.

Pritchell: A small hammer-punch used by smiths and farriers.

Rods: The horizontal woven hazel twigs of a wattle hurdle.

Sails: The upright pieces in a wattle hurdle.

Shell auger: A spoon bit with a crossed handle, used by the wheelright.

Shores: Upright posts at either end of a hurdle.

Shutting: A term used by blacksmiths to denote welding.

Slice: The long-handled shovel used for stoking the blacksmith's forge fire.

Sluing: A basket-weaving term, when two or more rods are woven together between uprights.

Spar hook: The splitting tool used in thatching to make the spars.

Spars: Pegs used in thatching to secure the straw or reed in position.

Spikes: Dags or fixing nails.

Splitting knife: A knife used for splitting wood held in a vice; also called a throe or froe.

Spokeshave: A two-handled blade used for shaving wood, also made with an open blade and known as a draw-shave or draw-knife.

Spurs: The lower smaller rods which are interwoven in the base of a wattle hurdle.

Stabbers: The upright stakes cut back in the hedge in the hedging process.

Stock-knife: A long-handled chopping knife with a hook at one end which fixed in an eye on a bench, used in clog-making. Various types include the hollowing knife and the morticing knife.

Stocks: The centres of wagon or cart wheels, made of elm.

Stowl: A term used in hedging referring to the hedge sending out shoots; also called tillering.

Strake: A term in thatching for a section of the roof.

Strakes: Iron tyres in double sections.

Strouters: Iron or wooden supports at the side of a wagon body.

Throe: Splitting knife (q.v.).

Throughs: The flat stones used as ties in dry walling.

Tillering: The partial cutting of the hedging briars to angle them for the hedging process.

Trace chains: These are used when a trace or extra horse is attached in tandem to the shaft horse.

Traveller: A measuring instrument used by the wheelwright.

Tree: The beechwood and metal framework of a saddle.

Tug hooks: These are fixed to the neck collar of a trace horse and trace chains link it to the shafts of the vehicle.

Twillies: Twisted rods in a wattle hurdle, helping to reinforce the twilly hole.

Twilly hole: The square hole made in a wattle hurdle for carrying it.

Twister: See *Bond twister*.

Wale: The cloth-lined underside of a horse's collar.

Winkers: The eye pieces on a draught bridle.

Yealm: A bundle of straw for thatching.

Yealming or **Yolming:** Drawing out straws for thatching.

Bibliography

Arnold, James. *The Shell Book of Country Crafts*. John Baker, 1968.

Bailey, Jocelyn. *The Village Blacksmith*. Shire Publications, 1977.

Bailey, Jocelyn. *The Village Wheelwright and Carpenter*. Shire Publications, 1975.

Blandford, Percy W. *Country Craft Tools*. David & Charles, 1974.

Fearn, Jacqueline. *Thatch and Thatching*. Shire Publications, 1976.

Hasluck, Paul. *Saddlery and Harness Making*. Cassell, 1906. Reprinted J. A. Allen, 1962.

Jenkins, J. G. *Traditional Country Craftsmen*. Routledge, 1965.

Legg, E. *Country Baskets*. Mills Boon, 1940.

Manners, J. E. *Country Crafts Today*. David & Charles, 1974

Niall, I. *Country Blacksmith*. Heinemann, 1966.

Rainsford-Hannay, F. *Dry Stone Walling*. Faber, 1965.

Smith, D. J. *Discovering Horse-drawn Commercial Vehicles*. Shire Publications, 1977.

Sparkes, Ivan G. *Old Horseshoes*. Shire Publications, 1976.

Sparkes, Ivan G. *Woodland Craftsmen*. Shire Publications, 1977.

Stowe, E. J. *Crafts of the Countryside*. Longmans Green, reprinted 1973.

Sturt, George. *The Wheelwright's Shop*. Cambridge University Press, 1963.

Tylden, Major G. *Discovering Harness and Saddlery*. Shire Publications, 1971.

Tylden, Major G. *Horses and Saddlery*. J. A. Allen, 1965.

Vince, John. *Discovering Carts and Wagons*. Shire Publications, second edition 1975.

Woods, K.S. *Rural Crafts of England*. Harrap, 1975.

Wright, Dorothy. *Baskets and Basketry*. Batsford, 1959.

The Blacksmith's Craft. CoSIRA, 1968.

The Thatcher's Craft. CoSIRA, 1961.

Index